Exeter Civic Society 1995

Discovering Exeter

Lost Churches by David Francis

1. *St David's* by Joyce Greenaway (1981)

2. *St Leonard's* by Gilbert Venn (1982)

3. *Heavitree* by Trevor Falla (1983)

4. *Pennsylvania* by Hazel Harvey (1984)

5. *Sidwell Street* by Hazel Harvey (1986)

6. *West of the River* by Hazel Harvey (1989)

7. *Lost Churches* by David Francis (1995)

Foreword

For centuries Exeter's population lived mostly within its walls; the many parish churches stood alongside the busy traders, the market stalls, workshops and inns that [...] the colourful street-scene, and the parish b[...] ntricate jigsaw. Curiosity about [...] been expressed by family [...] are now here displayed [...] student here. All profit [...] conservation work in [...] olomew Street – there is [...] – see within.

Hazel Harvey, Chairman.

© Exeter Civic Society

ISBN 0 9505873 5 4

Front cover – the nineteenth-century St David's church

Introduction

There were Christians in Exeter in Roman times (a cooking-pot has been found with a chi-rho mark) and Christian burials from the Dark Ages uncovered in the Cathedral Close show that Exeter has an unbroken tradition of 1,600 years of Christian practice. Celtic missionary saints founded churches; Saxon incomers built others. All the upheavals in the history of the church have played upon this stage: Exeter has seen pilgrims, pious bequests, two Protestant martyrs, a siege in the Prayerbook Rebellion, Quakers and Methodists tormented, the Oxford Movement, and constant changes in architectural fashion (even the great Norman cathedral was soon rebuilt in Gothic style). History shouts at every turn in Exeter. Countless reminders of past glories and ancient suffering can be found. The tale of the lost churches illuminates the long life of the city.

There is still a fascinatingly large number of little churches to be found in or near Exeter city centre. In days gone by, there were even more. Two parish churches, those dedicated to St James and St Cuthbert, had ceased to function by the fourteenth century. Allhallows-on-the-Wall, disused since the Civil War, disappeared altogether in the eighteenth century, and although it was replaced in the next, the nineteenth century saw the loss of St George's and St Kerrian's. Allhallows, Goldsmith Street, followed early in our century, with St Mary Magdalene's, St John's, St Paul's and the new Allhallows-on-the-Wall going in the 1930s. The war accounted for St Lawrence's and the Bedford Chapel. St Edmund's saw its last regular services in the 1950s, and St Mary Major and Holy Trinity had closed their doors to worshippers for the last time by the end of 1970. Even the replacement tower commemorating the site of St Kerrian's has now gone. Happily, the future of those churches that remain looks secure, even if they are not now all used regularly for worship. This little work seeks to record something of all those city centre churches that have gone, before their memory fades completely. So come with us on a tour of the faithful city, and we'll evoke those lost churches; most were of very ancient foundation, and their appearance will have changed much over the centuries as they were repaired or rebuilt; mostly, we shall be 'seeing' them as they were in their most recent guise.

The illustrations come from the author's private collection except where otherwise acknowledged. The copyright holder of the illustration on page 10 has proved impossible to trace.

Except for brief excursions west and east to consider St Edmund's and St Sidwell's respectively, our walk is limited to the churches or chapels that were within the old city walls. We are confining ourselves to Anglican establishments, or those that had disappeared by the end of the Reformation. Still extant churches receive an honourable mention in passing, as do those of the other denominations.

The SOCIETY for the PROTECTION of ANCIENT BUILDINGS

DESIRES TO REMIND THE
CITIZENS OF EXETER
THAT
THE FATE OF SOME OF THEIR
ANCIENT CHURCHES

WILL BE DECIDED AT THE PUBLIC INQUIRY TO BE HELD BY THE ECCLESIASTICAL COMMISSIONERS UNDER THE UNION OF BENEFICES MEASURE (1923) AT 11 O'CLOCK IN THE MORNINGS OF

JANUARY 21st & JANUARY 26th,
at the CHAPTER HOUSE OF THE CATHEDRAL

AND

IT ASKS THOSE WHO WISH TO ENSURE THE PRESERVATION OF THE CHURCHES OF

ST. PAUL, ST. JOHN and ST. LAWRENCE,
TO SECURE A HEARING OF THEIR VIEWS THEN, FOR IT WILL BE THEIR
LAST CHANCE TO DO SO.

A. R. POWYS,
Secretary.

Perhaps someone will one day write an itinerary of the latter, past and present. A tour of the existing churches is available from Exeter City Council's Guided Tour Service. And enough has been written about the Cathedral to obviate discussion here.

Note: Full details of books and articles referred to in the text by author's name will be found in the bibliography at the end.

Cresswell mentions an instruction from William the Conqueror to the Provost of Exeter to pay 1d out of city tolls to twenty-nine churches, (but she gives no reference).

The earliest list of names of churches is an ordinance of Bishop Marshal, (Chapter Manuscript 2923) which Rose-Troup quotes in full and dates from evidence of some of the persons therein mentioned as c.1200. The churches listed are those which belonged to the chapter: Holy Trinity, St James, St Michael, St Mary Major and St Mary Minor, St Petrock, SS Simon and Jude, St Martin, Christ Church, St Kerrian, St Cuthbert, Allhallows [on-the-Wall], St Clement, St David, St Sidwell, St Michael Heavitree and St Margaret Topsham.

Both Cresswell and Rose-Troup quote from a grant of one Peter de Palerna, which the latter dates as c.1214. Peter stipulated that 1d should be paid annually to twenty-eight churches: St Sidwell, St Bartholomew, St Stephen, St Martin, St Peter Major, (presumably the Cathedral), St Mary Major, St Mary Minor, St Peter Minor, St Petrock, St James, Holy Trinity, St Mary Magdalene, St Leonard, St George, St John, St Edward, St Edmund, St Thomas, Allhallows, St Olave, St Mary [Arches], St Cuthbert, St Kerrian, St Pancras, St Paul, Holy Trinity, Allhallows [Goldsmith Street] and St Lawrence. Only ten overlap with the chapter list, so we already have references to 35 churches and chapels.

The usual explanation of why Exeter had so many churches in a relatively small area is that when the invading Saxons reached this far west in about 660, they found the town already Christianised. The Saxons left the churches of the native British alone, and built others for themselves. By and large, the British part of the town was to the north of what is now Fore Street and High Street (typified by the dedications to the Celtic St Kerrian, and St Paul, the Breton St Pol de Léon), and the Saxon area to the south.

Moreover, in the early middle ages wealthy landowners or merchants, or small groups of them, would often found a church for their families and retainers. It is quite likely that, in a prosperous town like Exeter, some of the churches started thus and eventually achieved parochial status; others would not have had the resources to survive, and so disappeared. Several in the immediate area of the Cathedral probably fell in this latter category. The decision as to which were to be parish churches seems to have been taken in 1222.

Chapels would have been attached to the many monasteries that abounded here. (Brice tells us that "Exeter was once so over-run with Monasteries, and the Vermin therein fed, that it obtain'd the Nickname Monkton".) Some of these survived in other guises to be recorded below.

A significant episode in the history of all religious establishments was the Dissolution of the Monasteries, begun in 1536 to boost King Henry VIII's finances by appropriating their land. Some of the early chapels may have disappeared then.

As the sixteenth century progressed, the Reformation, that is the period when churches in this country were compelled to give up the Roman Catholic faith for Protestantism, resulted in the disappearance of several chapels that had not gained the status of parish churches. Non-parochial establishments such as Chantry Chapels, Guild Chapels and the like smacked unacceptably of Catholicism.

Of those parish churches whose demise is known, St Cuthbert's and St James's were merged with neighbouring parishes in the thirteenth and fourteenth centuries respectively because of poverty;

Allhallows-on-the-Wall was damaged beyond repair in the Civil War; St George's and St Kerrian's disappeared in the nineteenth century, for street improvement and because of general dilapidation respectively; Allhallows, Goldsmith Street, was lost early this century, again for supposed street improvement. But the biggest single cause of loss of churches was a report by the Bishop's Commissioners in 1930, which recommended the closure and eventual demolition of (the new) Allhallows-on-the-Wall, St John, St Paul, St Lawrence, Bedford Chapel and St Mary Major. A full press transcript of the report and the not unnaturally vociferous subsequent comment and correspondence is filed in the Westcountry Studies Library. In the event, it was the war that finally disposed of St Lawrence and the Bedford Chapel, and St Mary Major survived another forty years. Holy Trinity became redundant in 1968, but another use has been found for the building.

So, having disposed of the barest of historical bones, let's be on our way.

To simplify some of the directions and positions referred to below, Fore Street-High Street-Sidwell Street are presumed to be on a west-east axis, and North Street-South Street on a north-south.

St Mary Major

We'll begin at the Cathedral – a good place to start, because there is evidence of Christian activity in this area for perhaps fifteen centuries. Stand at the west door, turn your back on the Cathedral itself and there, a few dozen yards in front of you, until as recently as early 1971, was a church dedicated to St Mary. The cross which once adorned its spire can now be seen on the grass. To distinguish this church from others in the city of the same dedication, this one was known as St Mary Major, (and in some documents, St Mary Michel, St Mary (the) More, or Sancta Maria de Turre). The church as illustrated (with its Rector from 1896-1905) was built 1865-7, but there had been religious activity on the site from a very early date.

The most up-to-date account of the early history of the site is John Allan's chapter *The origin of the cathedral and archaeology of the close* in *Exeter Cathedral: a celebration*, pp.29-35. After the modern church was demolished, archaeological investigation of the site took place. Extensive remains of Roman legionary baths were found, and there was evidence of a basilica and the forum of a Roman town. There was also evidence of what may well be Christian burials from about the end of the fifth century, suggesting that there may have been a building here used for Christian worship and funerals during the so-called "dark ages". There is known to have been a minster in Exeter at the end of the seventh century, where Boniface was educated, and it received considerable support from King Athelstan (924-39). (But Cresswell reports a tradition that the minster where Boniface was educated was located somewhere near the church of St Pancras.) Leofric was installed as first bishop of Exeter in a monastery church in 1050, and this served him and his successor Osbern Fitzosbern as their cathedral. The third bishop, William Warelwast, a nephew of William the Conqueror, began building the present cathedral in the second decade of the twelfth century. Archaeological evidence showed that there had been a Saxon building of considerably larger area than the medieval church of St Mary Major but otherwise on the same alignment.

John Allan presents strong arguments for this having been the Saxon minster, and first cathedral. Firstly, the chancel area had been reduced in size early in the twelfth century, strongly suggesting a reduction in status from cathedral to parish church with the new cathedral under construction. Secondly, this early church had a major cemetery; none of the other churches had a cemetery at that time, and the new cathedral is presumed to have inherited this monopoly from its predecessor. Thirdly, the Court of the Archdeacon of Exeter continued to be held in the church of St Mary Major, indicating a retention of some special status.

And consider the alignment of Stepcote Hill-Smythen Street, the main road in from the west until the eighteenth century. Continue

The Old St Mary Major (reproduced from George Townsend's 'The Old Church of St Mary Major, Cathedral Close' by kind permission of the Royal Albert Memorial Museum, Exeter.)

this across what is now South Street, and you have an ideal processional route for the Bishop to the west door of his then cathedral. (See the reproduction of the notice board that formerly stood on the site of St George's church, on page 13).

However, it must be stressed that these deductions are not necessarily irrefutable. Future scholarship may yet show that St Mary Major was always a distinct church.

The Victorian St Mary Major

Jenkins tells us that the medieval church consisted of a nave only, opening through a lofty gothic arch at the east end into a chancel that appeared older than the rest of the fabric. He mentions a small tablet depicting St Lawrence being martyred on a gridiron, and recounts a tradition that the chancel was once a chapel, unconnected with the church, dedicated to that Saint, and adds points about the architecture of the vestry to support this possibility. Cresswell describes "a rudely sculptured representation of the martyrdom of St Lawrence" on the west wall of the replacement church, and states that it had previously been on the outer wall near the east porch.

Three-fifths of the rood screen found its way to St Mary Steps (see illustration below) when the medieval church was demolished; (the remainder was used to divide off part of the south aisle in the new church to make a chapel). The tower was enormous. Jenkins describes it as more like the keep of an ancient castle than a bell tower, but states that neither history nor tradition could give an adequate reason why it was so huge. Whatever the original reasons, it provided a good look-out post for sentinels during the Civil War, commanding a view of the whole city.

There was until the end of the sixteenth century a tall steeple with a weather-cock; the latter blew down in 1580 and the steeple was removed not long afterwards. The noise of the wind blowing around this weather-vane is said to have badly disturbed Catherine of Aragon's sleep as she travelled from Plymouth to meet her future husband Prince Arthur, in the autumn of 1501.

The old church was the last resting place of the parents of Sir Walter Ralegh (Walter senior having been buried there on 23 February 1580-81, and Katherine some time in 1594). They had lived in nearby Palace Gate. Sir Walter himself expressed a desire to be buried "in Exeter church near my father and mother", but was in the event laid to rest in St Margaret's, Westminster.

The top of the Norman tower, which originally reached a height of some 80 feet, was taken down in 1768, reducing it by some 35 feet, and was replaced by a cupola, which can be seen in our illustration of the old church.

By the mid-nineteenth century, the old church was in need of increased accommodation as well as general improvement, and first thoughts in the 1850s were to restore the existing church. But this would have been too expensive, and have resulted in no gain in accommodation, so a completely new church was planned. A newspaper report of 6 December 1867 observed "consecration and re-opening services of this new temple will take place very shortly".

The replacement used stones from its predecessor, and was set somewhat to the west, to improve the vista of the west front of the Cathedral. The new church consisted of a nave, south aisle and chancel, with tower and spire at the west end, and with a south chapel separated from the aisle by part of the earlier church's rood screen (see above).

Published thoughts about the new St Mary Major are consistent in their disapproval: "Words cannot express the disgust inspired by this pretentious monstrosity" (*Rambles by Patricius Walker* – i.e. William Allingham, 1873); "one of the many well-intentioned mistakes from which our parish churches suffered in the last century under the name of 'improvement'" (Cresswell); "an obtrusive flaw" (Sharpe); "major only as a disaster to the effect of the Close as a whole", (Pevsner). Little offers a partial defence, describing the church as "much reviled, and with some justice, but its arcade of stone and marble is a good Victorian interpretation of Early English".

Changing religious habits, especially after the second world war, and the loss of much of the parish's population due to redevelopment meant that the church was used less and less, and the last regular Anglican service took place at Easter 1965. The building was then used by the congregation of the Mint Methodists while their church was being rebuilt. A final joint service of Anglicans and Methodists took place on 25 October 1970.

St Mary Minor

Our two thirteenth-century documents mention a **St Mary Minor**. Historians have tossed the location of this establishment around a good deal. Rose-Troup refutes an assertion often held in her time that the church referred to was St Mary Steps, and claims to disprove another suggestion that the tower referred to above in Sancta Maria de Turre was in fact the tower of St Mary Minor. Hoskins states categorically that it *was* St Mary Steps, but Orme in his *Exeter Cathedral as it was* confirms the location as having been near to St Mary Major, perhaps on the west side, and says that the two churches were united in 1285. Allan adds the point that there were other examples of two or more churches on a single axis to serve an Anglo-Saxon monastery, citing Glastonbury and St Augustine's, Canterbury, as examples.

St Mary Major's medieval parish boundaries were extremely curious; most of the parish lay south-west of what is now South Street, with only a narrow strip of land passing down Little Style connecting the church with the rest of its parish. (Little Style was once a way from the Close to South Street, passing immediately to the north of the block of old buildings called Three Gables, at the base of which can still be seen one block of masonry from the church. Little Style is now blocked by buildings in South Street). There were several other churches which might be thought to serve the area better, not least St George's.

St George

To reach the site of St George's, pass down Kalendarhay. This is partially blocked by the ruins of the Hall of the College of the Vicars Choral. One small portion of masonry from St George's exposed by the bombs of 1942 is somewhat incongruously preserved in the ruins of the Hall, whither it was moved in 1952. This surviving fragment incorporates pieces of Roman red tiles and an Anglo-Saxon doorway with alternate long and short stones. Local historian A W Everett argued in the *Express and Echo* of 26 November 1949 that the remains should not be resited across the street, being part of a wall "over 1000 years old,… the only remaining link with Saxon Exeter".

The church had stood on the opposite side of South Street, about six shops down from the corner.

St George's parish lay to the north of that of St Mary Major. Jenkins describes the church as "small, consisting of a nave, chancel, and small aisle under the tower…; the tower… is not decorated with either spire or vane; it contains a good ring of five bells, and also a clock without a dial". (Does this mean it only struck the hours?) Before 1740, there were only three bells. That year, the Bishop granted a licence for casting the three into five. Among its monuments, the church contained the Royal arms of Charles II, presumably to celebrate the Restoration of the King and the restoration of the church (it having been sold under the Commonwealth) to its proper function once more.

Notice Board on site of St. George's Church, South Street.

St George's is mentioned in Palerna's grant and it may well have had a tenth-century origin. The church was given a parish in 1222, but it was usually held together with the living of St John's, until it became a rectory in 1814. St George's was closed and demolished in 1843, in the dubious interest of road improvement (widening South Street). The Commissioners of Improvement had approached the Rector, the Revd John Kingdon Cleeve, with a view to altering the church. His terms were that they should provide one foot of land behind the church for every foot they took from the front; (one account suggests two feet at the back for every one they took from the front). These terms proved unacceptable to the Commissioners, so Mr Cleeve refused to allow them to touch any of the church in his lifetime. He died in 1842, so it could be argued, as he would probably have wished, that the church was demolished only over his dead body. Cresswell recorded the site in South Street as having been preserved, "neatly kept as a garden with a board placed there recording the history of the church and some interesting parochial details". It is reproduced on page 13.

Gravestones lined the path. The west wall was still visible in 1946, according to *Exeter then and now*, and the general outline was quite discernible until redevelopment in the 1960s.

The Exeter Flying Post of 3 December 1873 recounts an amazing story. It gives no date, but tells how one William Newcome was on his way to Cornwall to collect rents. He died suddenly in the New London Inn. His relatives expressed a wish that he be buried in a church in Exeter, so the undertaker, Robert S. Cornish (from the tone of the article, a well-known Exeter figure) "after seeing the authorities of many parishes", obtained permission from the rector and churchwardens of St George's for him to be buried there. A space was opened in the chancel, and "to their surprise [they] found… another coffin laid there [containing the remains of] no other than the father of the deceased gentleman". He had also died suddenly at the New London Inn on his way to Cornwall to collect rents! The article goes on prosaically to state that with the £5 burial fee, a new silver alms dish was purchased.

The same article observes that St George's was a "Puritanical" church, and that Dr Cleeve and his son were ardent Evangelicals.

After the demolition of St George's, the benefice was permanently united with that of St John's. The bells and memorials went from St George's to St John's (see below) and the bells eventually found another home in St Mark's church.

Sketch of St George's (reproduced by kind permission of Devon County Council Libraries – Westcountry Studies Library.)

St James

Remaining on the east side of South Street, walk to the corner of Palace Gate, noting the fine Roman Catholic Church of the Sacred Heart, and the Baptist church next door, in passing. In this area once stood a parish church dedicated to St James, perhaps on about the site of shop on the corner. Listed in Bishop Marshal's ordinance, and recorded as still being there in 1312, it had gone by 1387. The parish was small and poor, so it was amalgamated with that of Holy Trinity. (Rose-Troup, p. vi, refers to a Rental of c.1308 indicating that St James paid no rent to the Chapter, with a marginal note giving the reason as poverty).

Many streets in Exeter take their name from the church to which they lead (sometimes dropping the "Saint", e.g. Martin's Lane, Mary Arches Street, Paul Street); there is a James Court, the vestiges of an erstwhile James Street not far away, leading westwards off South Street, but this took its name from the dissenters' James's Meeting, called after King James II. (The Oxford English Dictionary defines 'Meeting' in this sense as "a nonconformist place of worship, a dissenting chapel or meeting-house").

Passing down South Street, note Global Village. This was formerly the Unitarians' George's Meeting, built about 1760. The building still contains a seventeenth-century pulpit reputedly originally

Holy Trinity

belonging to James's Meeting, and a fine late seventeenth- or early eighteenth-century clock, both sadly mutilated.

Sir John Bowring (1792-1862) describes in his *Autobiographical Recollections* how he attended George's Meeting as a child, amusing himself by staring at the letters S S entwined in the brass chandelier, and the slow-moving hands of the clock. "The two hands were the images of knowledge and faith. The progress of one I could trace from 'tick to tick' – of the other I could only convince myself that it had moved… if for a few minutes I turned my eye away". He also remembered the rising (or setting?) sun over the clock, and the gilded figure of Death which had lost the blade from its scythe. The thoughtful child grew up to help Jeremy Bentham draft the constitutions for Spain and Greece, to become Governor of Hong Kong, and to effect the introduction of the florin as the first step towards the decimalisation of British coinage, but he always regretted that he was unable to restore Death's scythe-blade.

George's Meeting closed as a chapel in 1983, and had been converted to commercial use (Global Village) by 1987. A number of local people have expressed their regret at how this fine old building has been allowed to be prostituted in this way, at least one describing it as "global pillage".

Continuing down South Street on the same side, we come to the White Ensign Club (for retired and active members of the Royal Navy and Royal Marines). This, from Christmas Day 1821 (the foundation stone having been laid on the site of the former church on 24 June 1819) until 21 January 1968 when the church was closed and the benefice united with that of St Leonard's, had been Holy Trinity Church. (For its predecessor, see below). There were originally small shops between the church and South Street, but realignment in 1958 cleared them away. Externally it has changed little, except for a general smartening up, (there was a sapling growing from the roof in the 1960s!).

Cresswell is very scathing about its "architectural deformities". Internally, it was rectangular, with four clustered columns supporting the galleries (removed c.1919), and more or less incidentally forming two aisles. There was a stone screen at the west end added in 1884 when the church also acquired tiled flooring and open seats. The pulpit was particularly lofty.

A number of memorials were brought from the old church (see below). Since its conversion to a social club, the building has been divided horizontally. Before that, it served as a warehouse for a time, and was threatened with demolition before the club took it over.

The earlier Holy Trinity Church

The earlier Holy Trinity Church, known to Peter de Palerna and perhaps dating from some 200 years earlier, had stood just inside the old South Gate. In the early years of the fifteenth century, the church was reroofed and the south and west walls rebuilt. Before this restoration, at least, it had a gallery, a high altar and three other altars, one dedicated to the Blessed Virgin and another to St Giles, of whom there was an image sculptured in wood and set in a tabernacle. There was also near the font a tomb with an effigy of John de Susseter, who became rector in 1349. Cresswell suggests that not all these items survived the restoration. In 1806, Jenkins saw it as "a handsome Gothic edifice". By then it had a tower with four untunable bells, and a clock with a dial, which impeded access to the gate. The church consisted of a chancel, nave, one aisle, separated by six clustered pillars (could the four in the later church have been salvaged from these?) and two galleries. It was demolished at the same time as the South Gate in 1819.

The South Gate had housed a prison. *The Exeter Flying Post* of 1 July 1819 recounts that after the laying of the foundation stone of the replacement church "forty gentlemen sat down to an excellent dinner at the Valiant Soldier Inn. Many loyal toasts were given; and some excellent songs, catches and gibes, kept up the festivity till a late hour. Forty workmen, employed about the building, were treated with a plentiful dinner, and a collection was made and sent over to the prisoners in the gaol; whom it was intended to have removed on that same day to the new Prison, but that was necessarily postponed and took place on Monday last". In other words, the poor prisoners rotted four extra days in the South Gate prison because the gentry and workmen got too merry celebrating the laying of the foundation stone of the church!

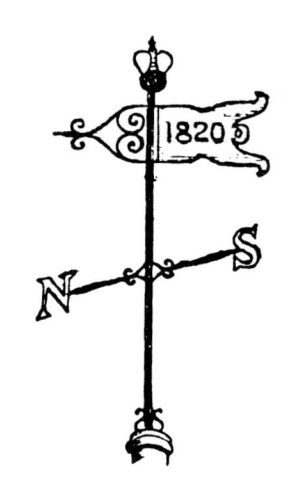

Vane, Trinity Church, South Street.

St Roche

Cross over South Street, and walk northwards again to Coombe Street, opposite Palace Gate. This has now been bisected by Western Way, but somewhere about where the eastern part now ends once stood a chapel dedicated to St Roche. Little is known about it except that it was built c.1400, soon after the death of Roche. It is thought to have been redundant by the 1590s, but may have survived physically for another century or so.

Coombe Street was sometimes referred to as Rock Street, indicating the pronunciation of the name of this Saint, who was invoked against pestilence and skin disease. He was a French hermit and pilgrim, c.1350-c.1380. On a visit to Italy he cured many cases of plague by miraculous means, but eventually caught it himself. He was fed by a dog, and recovered, but he was not recognised when he reached home and was imprisoned. Another tale has him imprisoned as a spy in Lombardy, where he died, and where miracles were attributed to his place of burial. His cult had something of a revival on the continent in the nineteenth century during serious outbreaks of cholera. St Roche's feast day is 16 August.

Down Coombe Street, on the left before the underpass, there is some waste land. This was the site of the Bonville Almshouses, founded by Lord Bonville in 1408 to house twelve poor people. Other almshouses in the city had their own chapel, so it is conceivable that St Roche's chapel could have been associated with them. Jenkins tells

St Mary Magdalene

us that material from the chapel was used to build tenements, but a superstitious tradition developed that no person ever prospered who inhabited them, and that they were pulled down and the site converted to a garden. Could this possibly explain why the area just above the underpass is still left empty?

It's difficult to know whether to spell Magdalen(e) with or without the final 'e'; recorded use varies so much. There's a letter from the then rector, Revd John Goundry, to the *Express and Echo* of 4 March 1935 which contains both forms!

Continue under the underpass into Lower Coombe Street, noting Quay Hill Evangelical Church, formerly St John's Tabernacle, on the left. At about the junction of Lower Coombe Street and Western Way once stood a church dedicated to St Mary Magdalene (not to be confused with a former chapel of that dedication at the hospital off Magdalen Road, about a quarter of a mile beyond the South Gate – presumably the St Mary Magdalene mentioned in Palerna's grant). This church is also sometimes referred to as St Mary's, Rack Street. It was consecrated on 24 September 1861 as a chapel of ease to St Mary Major, in what was then a densely populated, not to say slummy district. John Fowles, in chapter 36 of *The French lieutenant's woman*, set in 1867, graphically evokes the district: "… a distinctly louche area, rather away from the centre of town and the carbolic presence of the Cathedral. It occupied a part of the city that slopes down towards the river… a warren of streets still with many Tudor houses, badly lit, malodorous, teeming. There were brothels there, and dance-halls and gin-palaces… ".

Working this difficult patch reputedly sent the Revd Mortimer, pictured above under St Mary Major, to an early grave, and was responsible for one of his successors having a severe nervous breakdown.

Cresswell described the church as difficult to find, "hidden away in turnings between West Street and Rack Street". It consisted simply of a nave of four bays, chancel and north aisle, and was built of the usual red sandstone. Its services were very high, and initially it attracted fashionable people from other parishes, who took up the best seats, to the inconvenience of the poor parishioners for whom the church was intended. A local newspaper drew attention to this in the status-conscious terminology of the 1860s:- "As the church is intended for a certain class, that class ought to take precedence, and be the first to be accommodated. We earnestly hope, therefore, that this hint will be kindly taken by those for whom it is intended".

By the early 1930s, the church had outlived its usefulness, and the last service was held on Whit Sunday 1933. Discussions took place as to its possible use as a parish hall, or even using its material to build a church in another district, but these came to naught. A target for vandals, St Mary Magdalene's was eventually demolished in 1939. Some of its stones were used to build a new Lady Chapel for St James's Church which stood near the corner of St James's Road and Old Tiverton Road, but this was itself a victim of Hitler's bombs less than three years later.

St Mary Magdalene's church
(*photo courtesy the* Western Morning News.)

St Mary Steps

Proceed roughly westwards down Western Way, noting on your right the church of **St Mary Steps**, happily still in use, and full of interest. As we remarked above, this church acquired a large part of the screen from the old St Mary Major. The old screen stood at the top of the south aisle, and is just visible in our illustration. The five-bay screen at the top of the nave was a copy in design of the old screen, but not to the exact dimensions.

Interior of St Mary Steps; the part of the screen from the old St Mary Major can just be seen on the right. The rest of the screen is an imitation.

St Edmund

Now cross Western Way and follow the footpath down to the remains of St Edmund's church.

St Edmund's was last used regularly in 1956, although one service a year on St Edmund's day (20 November) took place there until 1968, conducted by the Rector of St Mary Steps, with which parish St Edmund's had been united. A serious fire in 1969 put an end even to this activity in the church, and, with new road construction, the remains (mainly the stunted tower) stand as a picturesque ruin on a roundabout.

The *Express and Echo* of 4 October 1975 tells how the workmen demolishing the unsafe portion of the tower uncovered a beer bottle left there by Frederick George Lendon and William S Sellick containing a penny and a halfpenny and a note dated 12 October 1935, reading "We have left under this bottle 1½d to be taken and held in trust by the finder. We sincerely hope he will not go rash and get drunk…".

The remnant we see today is in fact of the third church dedicated to St Edmund on or near this site. The first was probably a very small chapel taken down when the first stone Exe Bridge was built c.1200. Its replacement was built on the piers of the causeway leading to the bridge itself. (There is a tradition that Edmund, a seventh-century king of East Anglia, hid under a bridge after his battle at Hoxne against the Danes; hence the dedication to St Edmund of several churches or chapels in various parts of the country situated on or near bridges). The church consisted of a nave and aisle with galleries at the west end and over the aisle. It had a small tower and spire with a weather vane. According to Jenkins, there were six bells, (although Cresswell's findings suggest only five – see below) and "a good clock with a chime". He comments on how well-kept the interior of the church was. This tower was struck by lightning in 1800 and the clock dial shattered.

The old St Edmund's.

With the opening of the new Exe Bridge in 1778, St Edmund's was, to use a modern expression, "marginalised". Probably because of increasing dilapidation, (or, according to one more cynical suggestion, a little dilapidation providing the excuse to completely rebuild), it was demolished and rebuilt in 1833-4. The tower was partially retained, having been repaired with an ornamental parapet. An oak screen at the west end divided an ambulatory from the rest of the church, which was rectangular in shape, with a west gallery. Cresswell describes the seating as being chairs in the centre of the church, with open benches at the sides which came from the Cathedral. Apparently the font from the old church was lost and a new octagonal one in gothic style substituted. This stood under the gallery, to the north-west. Some time after 1906, the font from Allhallows, Goldsmith Street also found its way to St Edmund's; *Exeter then and now* describes this font as "small and graceful" and gives its location as "at the other side", presumably meaning nearer the south door. Cresswell lists eight bells, five of the eighteenth century and three dated 1833.

The post-card from which our interior view is taken is dated St Edmund's rectory 31 January 1936 and bears the following intriguing message: "The article worked out pretty well… made a few people think down in these parts". It is signed simply 'P'. The rector at the time was the Revd Frank Urwin, so who was P, and what was s/he making people think about?

St Edmund's interior.

St Edmund's exterior.

St Edmund's Lady Chapel.

24

St Mary (on the Bridge)

There was also a medieval chantry chapel dedicated to St Mary on the bridge, (almost opposite St Edmund's) and it is here that the patron of the first Exe Bridge, Walter Gervase, was reputedly buried. Certainly, bones were found there when the chapel was demolished in 1833.

In 1656, under the Commonwealth, all but four of Exeter's churches were ordered to be sold and used as burying places or schools, and the various parishes united. Along with those of St Petrock, St Mary Major and St Mary Arches, St Edmund's was retained. Most of the churches were eventually bought back by their parishioners, but the next church we meet, Allhallows-on-the-Wall, was the only one that did not subsequently come back into use.

Allhallows-on-the-Wall

Proceed across the medieval bridge, recalling that the original St Thomas's church stood at the other end before it was moved to its present position to avoid frequent flooding. (see *West of the River*, No 6 in this series). Turn right into New Bridge Street. The building behind the shop line on the left was formerly a Pentecostal Chapel. Its entrance is still visible in the red-brick building with a classical doorway with an open book in the plaster decoration of the pediment opposite the stone balustrade of New Bridge Street.

As noted above, the first bridge across the Exe was built around 1200. This gave directly on to Stepcote Hill. To provide easier access to Fore Street/High Street, the bridge on which you are now walking was opened in 1778. From sometime in the twelfth century, there stood at the bottom of what is now Fore Street where the line of West Street and Bartholomew Street cross it, a church called Allhallows-on-the-Wall, in Latin Omnes Sancti supra Murum or Muros – it varies between singular and plural in various sources, – (the Latin "supra" probably meaning here "higher than", rather than strictly "on top of"). The church seems to have been positioned at right angles to the wall, giving it (approximately) the "correct" east-west alignment.

Jenkins states that the large and lofty square tower, built of reddish stone, appeared to have been erected as an additional defence to the city walls; indeed, Royalist forces had placed a cannon on it during the siege 1645-6, resulting in the destruction of the church, but ironically not of the tower itself, by the Parliamentary forces. The gaping roofless ruin was not finally cleared away until about 1770, in preparation for the construction of the new bridge. The parish was united with that of the still extant St Mary Steps.

The shop on the south-west corner of West Street and New Bridge Street has cellars underneath with large iron doors opening into what are thought to be the ovens of a bakery that at one time stood here. The ovens open into what was the crypt of the old church.

Now turn left and walk along Bartholomew Street, noting the fine early nineteenth-century Baptist Chapel, and follow the road round to the right, to the grassed open space. In a flurry of nineteenth-century piety, a new Allhallows-on-the-Wall, (sometimes referred to as Allhallows, Bartholomew Street and in one case – a map in Sharp – as St Bartholomew's !) was built here, in what was known as Bartholomew Yard.

This was a "new" cemetery opened in 1647 because the original one around the Cathedral was full. So, curiously, when the new Allhallows-on-the-Wall opened, it had a ready-made and already full grave-yard! The name "Bartholomew" had been given because the cemetery was consecrated on St Bartholomew's day. This cemetery was in turn full by 1837, when the catacombs and extension of the cemetery down the hill were brought into use.

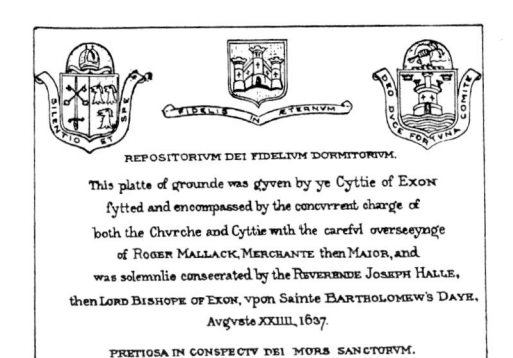

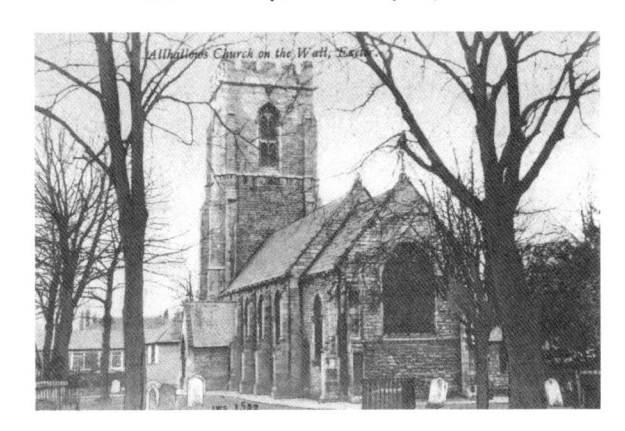

Allhallows-on-the-Wall exterior.

The new church was designed by local architect John Haywood. Its foundation stone was laid on April 4th 1843, (the year St. George's was demolished – did someone have a conscience?) and the church was consecrated on September 22nd 1845. Built of limestone, it had an embattled west tower finished with pinnacles. These weathered so badly that they were removed in 1902. Access to the church was through a west door or south porch, where one would find the nave divided from the chancel by a light screen of wrought iron, surmounted by a cross. Cresswell thought the windows poor, the period being "one of the worst periods of coloured glass", but she admired the font "in the modern Gothic style". This new Allhallows was of the high church persuasion, and was the first in Exeter to have a daily celebration of the Eucharist. It served its flock until 1938, (the living being held in plurality with that of St John's since 1931), when it was deemed redundant. The former church operated as a factory producing corsets and parachutes for a time, but various suggestions for its long-term secular use came to nothing, and it was finally demolished in 1950.

Allhallows-on-the-Wall interior when in use as a corset factory (photo courtesy Mrs G Price).

The gate in the surrounding wall is still present. All Hallows Court has been built subsequently just to the west of where the church was, and the damaged remains of the font can still be seen in the grass there.

In 1866 the rector, the Revd John Gilberd Pearse, founded a sisterhood called the Community of St Wilfrid, at a house in Bartholomew Street. At the time, it was the only such religious community in Exeter. The sisters ran an orphanage (which moved into the rectory at what was 29 St David's Hill in 1904), and a school at the Bartholomew Street premises, among their many other good works. The orphanage closed in 1954, and in 1966 the convent moved to Duryard Grange, and then to Culverland Close, off Union Road. A dwindling group of aged nuns is still there in 1995.

St Mary and St Francis

Before we leave this site, we may reflect that in medieval times there was a Franciscan Friary with its own chapel dedicated to **St Mary and St Francis** in this same stretch of open space. Although the Friars eventually moved to new premises beyond the South Gate, their chapel remained until c.1500.

Assumption of Our Lady

Now go along Friernhay Street, turn right and walk as far as the Tuckers' Hall. Many trade guilds in Exeter had highly religious-sounding names. The cordwainers were the Fraternity of the Blessed Trinity, the bakers the Fraternity of St Clement, and the tailors the Fraternity of St John the Baptist. The Guild of Weavers, Tuckers and Shearmen were known as the Fraternity of the Assumption of the Blessed Virgin Mary. In 1471 their Chapel of the **Assumption of Our Lady** in the parish of St John was built. They were the only guild to have a hall used for religious as well as secular purposes, although it was not until 1523 that it was officially recognised by the religious authorities as a chapel. Even then, nothing was to be done that would disadvantage the parish church of St John. The chapel was at the east end, screened off from the west end, where secular business was conducted. It later became simply a meeting house for the guild, probably soon after the reformation, but certainly by 1602.

St John

Let's now make our way back to the end of Friernhay Street. Across the road, on the corner of the still extant John Street is the site of St John's Church. Cresswell notes that tradition had it dedicated to St John the Evangelist, but noted that such dedications were very rare in medieval times and thought it more likely to have been originally dedicated to St John the Baptist.

The church was known to Peter de Palerna. The *Express and Echo* of 10 July 1933 referred to "last evening's service, which may prove to be the last". Redundancy was confirmed the following year. The church was largely demolished in 1937 (the work continuing into 1938), although the tower survived another 20 years. Some pre-fifteenth-century work was found on demolition, but the church had been largely rebuilt, and extended southwards in 1791. Before 1863, the chancel was in a bow over the contiguous John Street – indeed, the church was often referred to as St John's Bow. (A similar arrangement still exists in St Stephen's, although the space in the bow, formerly the chancel, is now used as a meetings room.) The bow provided the cart entrance to Butchers' Row. St John's lost its bow in 1863, again in the supposed interests of street improvements, and an east wall and window were substituted. Every Michaelmas since the Dissolution, the rector had paid three pounds fourteen shillings and fourpence-halfpenny to the Duchy of Cornwall, believing this to be rent paid for a bow over a public street. He thus thought that the payment made at Michaelmas 1862 should be the last. But the Office of Woods and Forests South West discovered in 1866 that the money was payable to the Crown, and therefore still due.

The tower stood in the north-east corner. The entrance was in the north wall.
Before 1778, the slope of what is now Fore Street (then High Street) in front of St John's was less steep, the gradient increasing more suddenly a little further down. In order to make access to the new bridge easier, the gradient was reduced by setting it back eastwards. But this resulted in only the vestry and tower door of the church being level with the street, – the rest was "upstairs". (There was a time when the vestry was used as a cobbler's stall). Another result was that the foundations were exposed, and seriously weakened.

A feature of St John's was the enormous lighted clock that projected, at third storey level, well out over the pavement. There was a period in the nineteenth-century when this clock had two minute hands, one showing "railway" time, the other about twenty minutes behind showing Exeter time, a reminder that until the standardisation of clocks necessitated by railway timetables, each locality took its time from the sun. One minute hand was reputedly golden, the other silver, but which was which is now uncertain.

An old view of St John's church.

Fore Street showing the church and clock.

Internally, there was little of great interest, the erstwhile chancel in the bow having been replaced by a simple sanctuary. South and west galleries were added in 1843, to cope with the additional congregation from the former St George's. The pulpit, on the north side of the sanctuary, had been exceptionally high to enable the preacher to see into the galleries, but was subsequently considerably lowered. St John's had only one bell before the closure of St George's, when the five from that church were added. Cresswell commented on the brass cross and flowers on the altar, "showing that care is bestowed on the sanctuary of a church which in appearance must be the despair of any incumbent". This last clause makes an interesting contrast with a comment in the *Western Morning News* for 6 January 1936: "… it is such an architectural jewel as no city with a proper sense of values would allow to disappear".

At demolition, the memorials were taken to St Mary Major, and the bells happily found a new home in St Mark's church.

A quaint custom that survived as long as the church was the provision of an oaken snuff box on the table at Vestry meetings for anyone who wished to partake.

Before leaving this location, look down John Street, as it were under the old bow. The shop you can see stands on the site of Bow Meeting, another dissenting establishment there from about 1620 to 1820. John Street wasn't always as featureless as it is today. A correspondent to the *Express and Echo* of 14 June 1982 recalled a local man harking back to a time when you could get married, pawn the ring and get drunk in the pub all without leaving John Street.

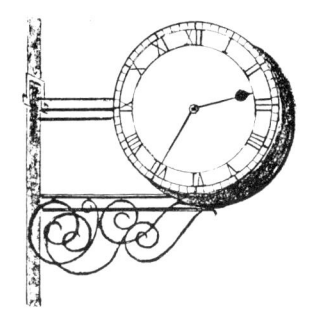

Head of stackpipe, St. John's Church, Fore Street.

St Nicholas

Continue up Fore Street and turn left into the Mint. There's a little public garden, just before you reach the remains of St Nicholas's Priory, founded in 1080. This is the site of the Priory church.

It is recounted that in 1321 the belfry fell in. Relations between the Dean and Chapter of the Cathedral and the monks of the Priory were so bad that it was the Bishop of Bath and Wells rather than the Bishop of Exeter who granted indulgences to all who would contribute to the rebuilding.

The Priory church was the scene of a violent incident with comic overtones in the summer of 1535, during the Dissolution. Royal commissioners had been sent to examine the affairs of all the religious houses. They had instructed a workman to remove the roodloft, and then promptly adjourned for lunch. Several women of the district, probably members of the poorer classes who had been glad of the food and drink they received from time to time at the Priory and resenting its destruction, broke into the church using such tools as they could lay hands on. The unfortunate workman had to jump from a window to dodge the hail of stones directed at him, narrowly avoiding breaking his neck, but sustaining a broken rib in the process. An Alderman, John Blackaller, tried with sweet talk to pacify the women, but to no avail, and was sent packing by a blow from one Elizabeth Glandfield. The Mayor, anxious that news of this event should not reach the commissioners, then appeared on the scene with his officers. The women had locked themselves in, and the Mayor and his men had to break in to arrest them. Only then did the commissioners come to hear of the incident. They thanked the Mayor for his efforts on their behalf, but asked that the women should be released.

The Priory was duly abolished, and stones from the erstwhile chapel were used to repair the Exe Bridge after one of its middle arches had collapsed in November 1539, fulfilling an ancient prophecy that one day the Exe would flow beneath St Nicholas.

Opposite the Priory is a late eighteenth-century former Roman Catholic Church, also dedicated to St Nicholas. The presbytery and Sunday School buildings are quite apparent, but the church building itself, full of features of interest, is difficult to see, being behind a wall. It may be that future developments in this area will afford a view of the church, but at the time of writing (April 1995) no specific plans were in train.

St Olave, St Mary Arches

Go back into Fore Street, noting the Mint Methodist church in passing. Continuing eastwards, inspect **St Olave's**, still used for worship. Down the eponymous street (without the prefix Saint) you'll find **St Mary Arches** church, war damaged, but repaired and still in use as the Exeter Diocesan Education Office. This is thought to be the only church in Devon to retain its Norman arches, and it was one of the four that were to be retained under the Commonwealth. Most of its ecclesiastical features remain. To see inside St Mary Arches it is best to go on the churches tour run by the City Council's Guided Tour Service. One remarkable artefact is the processional cross usually kept to the north of the altar. Its handle is badly charred. This was a result of its catching fire when the roof was set ablaze in the blitz. The nuns of St Wilfrid's rescued it, still burning, and were able to douse the flames.

St Mary Arches exterior

St Mary Arches interior.

Mary Arches Lane (as it was then) was the principal route to St Bartholomew's Yard, and is given a spooky evocation by Brice:
"No maudlin bibbers… /
In Mary Arches Lane… /
See Coffins op'ning or White Shrouds to stalk
Or Palls or Cloaks in black Procession walk…
No Headless-Horse neighs strolling Wench to Bed…
The Waits may now, in blackest Month , go through
Ev'n the suspicious Close of BARTHO'MEW."

Brice himself may have been laid to rest by this route. He was interred in St Bartholomew's Yard in November 1773, to a musical accompaniment.

Behind St Mary Arches is the Synagogue, built about 1835, with its impressive Greek Doric entrance.

Pass back into Fore Street, continue eastwards to North Street.

The east corner of the junction of North Street and High Street used to be known as St Peter's Corner. It was so named because a statue of Saint Peter, reading a bible and trampling on a pagan, had stood in various niches and at various heights on this corner over the centuries. The statue is now in the Royal Albert Memorial Museum.

Brice describes St Peter's Corner thus:
"By this, where Houses, whelving, Houses meet,
And vault with Beetle-brows a shelving Street,
Where stout St PETER, on the Corner stall,
Props the impending Edifice from Fall… "

Jenkins recounts that on midsummer's eve, there was a spectacular procession involving the mayor, citizens and trade guilds. Each of the guilds was preceded by a life-size statue of their tutelar saint (see above under **Assumption of Our Lady**). St Peter was the patron saint of the fishmongers. At one time, similar statues were mounted at the other three corners of the Carfoix.

The story is told of an old Exeter character known as Artful Thomas who would stand gazing at the statue, convincing passers-by that the Saint was about to turn over the page of his bible; when a sizeable crowd had gathered, he would quietly disappear, leaving them with acute neck-ache and embarrassment.

St Kerrian

Come down North Street, on the east side. **St Kerrian's** church, another of those listed in 1200, stood about mid-way along where the ramp leads up into the shopping precinct. This church was demolished in 1878, although a replacement red sandstone tower containing the original clock to mark its location was built in 1880 and survived until 1970. An associated notice is reproduced.

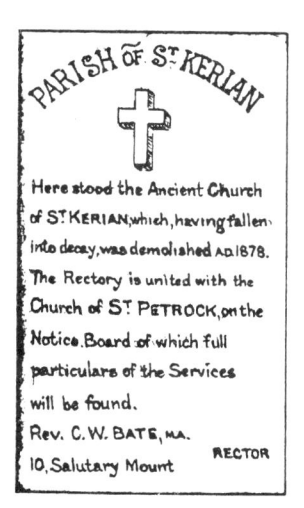

> PARISH OF ST KERIAN
>
> Here stood the Ancient Church of ST KERIAN, which, having fallen into decay, was demolished A.D. 1878. The Rectory is united with the Church of ST PETROCK, on the Notice Board of which full particulars of the Services will be found.
>
> Rev. C. W. BATE, M.A. RECTOR
> 10, Salutary Mount

It will be noticed that the spelling of Kerian there is with one 'r', and the Latin is "Capella Sancti Kerani", but elsewhere Kerrian is usually spelled thus, with the double 'r'.

35

There is also some confusion over the dedicatee. Cresswell says that he was the patron Saint of Cornish tin miners, i.e. the same person as St Piran or Perran, who gives his name to Perranporth and other places in the Duchy. But the Oxford Dictionary of Saints (1978) rejects this. Its entry on Kerrian (with the double 'r') states: "a British male saint culted in Cornwall, Brittany, and at Exeter (Leofric Psalter and church dedication). Once wrongly identified with the Irish Ciaran". Its entry under that Saint (a fifth- or sixth-century Irish monk and bishop) says that identification of him as Saint Perran, prevalent since medieval times, is now considered wrong. Kerrian's feast day is unknown, but the feast days for Ciaran (of Saighir) and Perran are the same – 5 March. It would be interesting to discover when the parishioners of St Kerrian's celebrated their patronal festival.

The church had disappeared by the time Cresswell made her survey, and Rose-Troup presumably considered its demise too recent to include in her study of lost chapels, so we are left largely with Jenkins's description – which is the sparsest of all his accounts of the churches as he found them!

He states that the church "is dark and gloomy, and from its not being used for divine service, little attention is paid to its interior part; the tower, which is over the entrance, is low, and contains one bell and a clock, with a dial fronting on the street". He makes no mention of the interior arrangements, and describes just one monument, "an excellent carving in bas-relief representing the resurrection at the day of judgement". This was apparently done by John Weston, fl. 1696-1733, an Exeter man whose church monuments are held to equal or surpass the finest London examples. Happily, this carving, erected to the memory of Jonathan and Elizabeth Ivie, is now preserved in St Petrock's church, immediately above the entrance porch.

The gloominess could not have been helped by the fact that there were buildings on three sides of the church. The chancel measured 18 by 18 feet with the nave at 30 by 18 feet. The west gallery was of painted Italian work, and there was a screen between the nave and the chancel, also of "once gaudy Italian work". There was apparently no font.

The living of St Kerrian's was usually held with that of St Petrock, at least since the Reformation.

St Cuthbert

St Cuthbert's appears on Bishop Marshal's ordinance, and was a parish church, located at the foot of North Street, probably just inside the City Walls by the North Gate, perhaps in the south west corner of what is now North Street and Bartholomew Street East, or perhaps within the gate itself. Because of the poverty of the parish and that of its neighbour, St Paul's, the two parishes were united in 1284/5. Meller tells us that the building survived to be demolished with the North Gate. This took place in 1769. If the church did disappear then, weight would be added to the surmise that the church was built into the gate itself. Have a look at the relief of the gate on the board, reproduced here.

There is a small cupola on part of the building, and this appears in other views of the gate. It may just be that this was the church.

John Wesley is reported to have preached in a room over the North Gate in 1762. Could this have been in what was once St Cuthbert's church? There is a parallel for Nonconformists taking over an ancient chapel elsewhere in the city – see below under Holy Trinity.

St Cuthbert is essentially a northern Saint, but it is known that King Alfred particularly venerated him, and Freeman suggests that he may have wished to commemorate Cuthbert for one of his victories locally over the Danes.

St Michael and All Angels

While in this part of the city, you may wish to detour to St Michael's, by far the most impressive church in the city, with its spire 220 feet in height. It is a chapel of ease to St David's, built in 1868 mainly to serve the neighbouring almshouses. But Mr William Gibbs of Tyntesfield, who defrayed the entire cost, decided on something more elaborate than a simple almshouse chapel, and St Michael's was the result. It was consecrated on 30 September 1868.

St David's itself had only been rebuilt in 1816. There is a story that the attention St Michael's received threatened to jeopardise the fortunes of the parish church, so yet another (the present) St David's was built at the end of the century.

St Paul

If you choose not to visit St Michael's, continue down North Street and turn right up Paul Street. If you have been to St Michael's, retrace your steps and turn left into Paul Street. Go along the south side underneath the footbridge to just beyond the traffic signs. Here Goldsmith Street used to make a junction, and St Paul's church stood in the south-east corner.

The dedication is almost certainly to the Breton-by-residence Saint Paul Aurelian, not St Paul of Acts of the Apostles fame; dedications to him are nearly always jointly with St Peter. This St Paul was the son of a British chief who lived in the sixth century. With twelve companions he migrated to Brittany where they founded a number of churches. He became Bishop of the place to which he gave the name, and by which he is also known, Saint Paul-de-Léon. His feast day is 12 March.

The church was there early in the thirteenth century, when the City of Exeter and Kalendar Brethren granted the canons of the Cathedral their rights at St Paul's in exchange for rights at St Mary Major. There was a St Paul's church on the site until 1936, when as Hoskins fulminates, it was "wantonly destroyed.... The then bishop (Cecil) authorised this vandalism... ". In partial defence, it should be pointed out that as a result of a slum clearance programme entailing the removal of the shops and dwellings on the north side of Paul

Street to make way for a bus station, there were very few residents left in the parish.

An old sketch of St Paul's.

The parish had been united with those of Allhallows, Goldsmith Street, and St Pancras in 1900. The last annual meeting took place on 10 April 1934, and the last service seems to have been in November that year. Some 306 corpses interred in the church were quietly removed and reburied in the Higher Cemetery. An important resident buried there in March 1703/4 aged 70 was Sir Edward Seaward, principal donor of Berry (now Bury) Meadow. He was governor of the workhouse which preceded the Royal Devon and Exeter Hospital at Heavitree; the latter has a ward named after him.

The church that was demolished in 1936 was a late seventeenth century replacement for what Jenkins describes as "the ancient church… dark, mean and in a ruinous state". Several authors have accredited it with some architectural merit. Jenkins describes it as "a handsome edifice… very neat withinside", Hoskins as "a delightful little seventeenth-century building", and Little as "simply classical in style and like one of Wren's less assuming London churches".

In spite of his praise for the design of the church, Jenkins criticises the architect who "grossly deceived the parishioners, by imposing on them a soft, sandy stone, which is greatly decayed, and though erected only about 120 years since, appears in a ruinous state, especially the cornices and ornaments in the front, the side next to the street having been recently repaired".

St Paul's exterior (Photo courtesy Peter Thomas – Isca Collection).

To some eyes, it looked more like a typical non-conformist chapel than any other Anglican church in the city centre. There is a story of one newly-appointed incumbent who walked up and down the road several times before recognising what was to be his church.

The main entrance was under the west tower, up a flight of steps. Inside, the church was rectangular, with a west gallery and black marble font. The tower contained a clock with one bell, and a small spire with a weathercock in Jenkins's time, when there was also a small graveyard. Both Cresswell and Jenkins refer to the large number of memorials in the church, the most famous person commemorated there being the painter William Gandy; at least some of these found their way to St Martin's church, and the screen went to St Paul's, Honiton, where it can still be seen.

The dedication to St Paul eventually passed to a new church on a green-field site in Burnthouse Lane.

St Pancras

An old view of St Pancras.

Continue up to Queen Street, and detour through the shopping precinct to visit the church of **St Pancras**. The pavement of the Roman praetorium was found nearby. St Pancras was venerated in the very early days of christianity so it is conceivable that a church has been here since Roman times.

Then come back to the end of Queen Street, and turn right into High Street. A short distance along, at the junction of High Street with the now pedestrianised Goldsmith Street, a plaque on the side of H Samuel the Jeweller tells us this was the site of:

Allhallows, Goldsmith Street

This was a particularly ancient, probably Celtic church. It was removed on the grounds that the street needed to be widened to give better access to the market, and that it was no longer necessary as the population of its parish had significantly declined. The last service took place on 10th December 1905, when the sermon was appropriately on the text "Little children, it is the last time" (1 John 2.18). The church was demolished the following year. The postcard which provides our illustration, dated 12 August 1906, includes the following in its message: "… this is the church you saw them taking down". The font went to St Edmund's and most of the other furnishings went to St Pancras's; the fine Jacobean pulpit, albeit somewhat reduced in size, and several memorials can still be seen there.

Jenkins gives the following dimensions: nave, 41 by 20 feet; chancel 15 by 12 feet (cf. St Pancras, which measures 46 feet by 16 feet). Unusually, Allhallows ran north-south, (rather than east-west) with the altar at the south end. The church had apparently been largely rebuilt in the fifteenth century, (although the chancel arch was said to date from 1380), and a tower was added to the south-west corner around 1546. The church was reseated and various furnishings were added in 1680, but it was little used throughout the eighteenth century. (No rector was instituted after the Revd Edward Bradford in 1683 until 1821.) The tower was found to be beyond

Allhallows, Goldsmith Street, exterior.

repair by 1767, and twenty feet of it was removed, to be partially replaced by a cupola containing one bell.

Jenkins says that the church was "small and gloomy, and not being made use of, is consequently dirty, and in bad repair within".

There were discussions about removing it in 1820, and uniting the parish with St Stephen's, but negotiations were so tardy that at length the parishioners resolved to restore their church and have regular services again. To this end, a rector was appointed in 1821. In 1822, a skylight in the roof was added, and a gallery inserted at the west end. Allhallows was one of the first churches in Exeter, if not the first, to use gas for lighting. Further improvements took place through the 1850s.

Closure again looked a possibility in 1864, when discussions took place on uniting the parishes of St Martin, St Stephen and Allhallows and building a new church to take the place of all three. Ominously, it was suggested that the removal of Allhallows and St Martin's churches would be an improvement to the streets in which they were situated. However, these discussions came to naught.

In 1680, one Peter Shapley, a goldsmith, had been granted a newly erected shop with a storey over, on the corner of High Street and

Goldsmith Street. This is presumably the house which "almost completely enveloped the chancel" of the church until the house was demolished in 1880. Its ground floor measured only 8 feet wide by 5 to 7 feet deep. The details about the house are recounted in James Crocker's *Sketches of old Exeter*, 1866. Crocker was one of those who helped restore the church in the 1880s.

Under the last rector, the Revd William Hope, instituted 1882, the flooring and seating were replaced, and in 1887, a new west wall, with a memorial window to the Queen's golden jubilee, was built. The rector had worked very hard in his time at Allhallows to raise the money to effect these improvements, and the church's closure and demolition must have been particularly galling for him.

Allhallows came back briefly to public attention at the end of 1979. The *Express and Echo* for 15 November reported that workmen digging the foundations of the new Marks and Spencer store unearthed six 300-year-old skeletons that had been built into the fabric of the old church.

Allhallows, Goldsmith Street, interior.

Ss George and John the Baptist, Guildhall

Let's pause here briefly to consider the Guildhall. What is now the Mayor's parlour, on the first floor in the porch over the pavement, was originally a chapel, dedicated to St George and St John the Baptist.

St Lawrence

We now continue eastwards up the High Street, on the north side, to the Co-op Bank. A plaque on the wall tells us this was the site of St Lawrence's church, here in 1214, and possibly pre-dating the Norman Conquest.

This was the only parish church within the old city walls to have been destroyed beyond repair by Hitler's bombs (on May 4 1942, the ruins finally being cleared in 1946). At the time of the bombing, most of the fabric of St Lawrence's was fifteenth-century or later, the south wall having been rebuilt in 1674 and the west wall in 1830. Brice complains that the street side of this south wall was too often used as a public privy; in his own well-chosen words: "It's a *Stinking Shame*, that, for Want of proper Palisades or Rails, this Church's Side is made a perfect Jakes of".

The church had an embattled south wall, and an embattled tower at the west end, with entrance via a south porch adjacent. (Jenkins states that the tower was finished with a coping wall without battlements, so these seem to have been a fairly recent addition). Brice states that the tower contained three bells; he didn't seem to think much of their musicality:

"The Bells (whose Match no Carrier's Fore-Horse e'er
Could, for capacious Size, presume to wear)
Their tingling Clappers, tripple Clink, imploy,
And ding-dong wrangle forth parochial Joy:
The treble Discord peals exact the same
To 'wail in doleful Clash a House in Flame."

His note is entertaining: "The Tower, built of red roughish Stone, being much larger than, though scarce so high as, many Chimnies, it's easy to suppose its Three Bells (for there are full so many) clashing make most excellent Musick. A Country Boy, passing with his Mother a while since by, and observing the Tower, innocently cry'd out 'Look, look, Mother, what a gurt Chimley that little House hath got'".

St Lawrence's figured picturesquely in eighteenth-century elections. On the buttress of the church was fixed a pole displaying a blue apron for a flag, whilst from the tower hung another apron of the same colour. From an early hour in the morning, a hogshead of cider was set up at the church for the use of the populace. Providing drink for the voters (quilling, as it was known locally, perhaps from the use of quills in the brewing process) was a well-known feature of elections at the time, but why these customs came into being particularly at St Lawrence's church is not clear. Perhaps it was something to do with the proximity of the castle, where the voting took place, but the hogshead of cider, at least, may explain why the wall of the church sometimes resembled a privy!

St Lawrence's exterior.

Our picture postcard illustration of the interior shows the nave, with the sanctuary divided from it by richly carved fifteenth-century woodwork said to have come from the cathedral. Jenkins and Cresswell mention a west gallery, but Jenkins adds in a note that another gallery, over the aisle, was erected in 1803. One wonders what aisle? Can he have meant the recess in the north-east corner where our illustration shows the organ? (This area was in earlier times a chapel, probably dedicated to Our Lady.)

St Lawrence's interior.

Cresswell describes certain memorials "on the south wall, just behind the pulpit". By the time our picture was taken, the pulpit had been moved to the north side, and the south wall apparently stripped of its memorials. She also describes the font as "perpendicular in style, and somewhat massive". It must have been a fairly recent addition to the church, for in 1842 a correspondent to *The Ecclesiologist* wrote "at the west end of this church is a large circular headed recess serving during service as a seat; on a bracket above is deposited a jar, like those in which dried leaves are kept, this thing, when there is a Baptism is brought down, set in the recess before mentioned, and serves as a font".

A curiosity was that while the north and south walls of the church were parallel to each other, the east and west walls both converged towards the north, so that geometrically, the church was a trapezium in plan. A small cemetery was added in 1692, accessible through a door on the north wall of the organ chamber.

In 1590, carvings in Beer limestone of Henry VIII and Elizabeth I were made by Arnold Hamlyn for a new fountain in the High Street, near St Lawrence's. The fountain, or conduit as it is often known, was demolished in 1694. Brice claims that the material was used to build the church's porch. The statue of Elizabeth was installed in an alcove over the entrance to the church, where it remained, even surviving the blitz. Offices of Commercial Union were built on the site of St Lawrence's, and the statue was displayed there. It duly moved with Commercial Union to Barnfield Road in the early 1973, but latterly it disappeared. It was traced to the company's store in Southampton, whence it was donated to the Royal Albert Memorial Museum following sterling efforts on its behalf by Peter Thomas. At the time of writing, the statue was on display at the entrance to the Underground Passages.

In medieval times there were certainly three, and probably four other chapels in St Lawrence's parish, and another nearby, in the Castle.

> This Churchyard Was Confecrated by ẙ R Rᵈ Jonathan Lᵈ B̃ᵖ of Exon And Giuen by Thomas Long B.D. for the benefit of the poore of Edward Clement and Robert Daw ẙ present Wardens and their succefsors Shall Thinke fitt (16 Charles Brimblecombe \92 Thomas Worth Colectors

Holy Trinity, Christ Church

Come back as it were past the west end of St Lawrence's church, to a point opposite the junction of Bedford Street and High Street. Until it was destroyed in the war in 1942, there was a Musgrave's Alley here, running parallel to Gandy Street. In earlier times, this had been referred to as Christ Church or Trinity Lane, and this betrays the existence of chapels of those dedications in this lane. (The lane was renamed to commemorate Dr William Musgrave, who practised there from 1690 to c.1730.)

Holy Trinity was there in 1200, perhaps originally a religious foundation with an almshouse. In the early fifteenth century, it was in the hands of the Fraternity of Shoemakers, and it survived the Dissolution, being repaired and enlarged by William Musgrave in 1694 and 1711. It became a Wesleyan Methodist Chapel known as Gidley's Meeting, from the efforts of a gentleman of that name who did much to secure it. John Wesley preached there in 1779. The Methodist congregation used it from about 1788 until their first service in the new chapel at the Mint on 25 March 1813. Rose-Troup says the chapel continued to be used by Dissenters until 1843; could this be a typographical error for 1813? It is still marked on the 1881 O.S. map, surveyed in 1876.

Latterly, at any rate, the chapel was on the first floor, over a warehouse. The entrance was on the corner nearest High Street and the stairs gave access to the middle of the south end. Northy quotes an old account which describes the pulpit "of goodly size, in which several persons could sit at once without at all incommoding the preacher". In the pews, the ladies sat at the right hand of the preacher, the gentlemen on the left.

Christ Church may have been built around the time of the Norman conquest. It is referred to separately from Holy Trinity in Bishop Marshal's ordinance but not in Palerna's grant, although various documents up to the fifteenth-century mention it (and the lane leading to it). The two chapels were evidently close together, and it is possible that latterly (in the fourteenth and fifteenth centuries) the two names were applied indiscriminately to one building. There is a precedent for this in Bristol, where Christ Church was sometimes called Trinity.

Rose-Troup in her sketch-map of the lost chapels places Holy Trinity the nearer to High Street and Christ Church further away. But she quotes a chapter rental (Chapter MS 3721) listing rent "de terre de criste churche a magno vico usque ad ecclesiam Trinitatis" ("from the land of Christ Church [which extends] from the High Street to the church of the Trinity"). Wouldn't this imply that Christ Church stood between Trinity and the High Street? Or could it have been that Christ Church owned land all the way round Holy Trinity?

On the O.S. map referred to above, Holy Trinity is shown about one building's width away from High Street.

OLD CHAPEL, MUSGRAVES ALLEY.

Holy Trinity interior.

Castle Chapel

The castle used to have a chapel dedicated to St Mary. A separate building within the castle complex consisting of a nave and chancel, it was founded some time in the first half of the twelfth century, and survived until the end of the eighteenth century – one source says 1774, another 1792. Freeman says it was a "small building", even smaller than a comparable chapel at Hastings.

The chapel stood close to the lodge, on the right as you enter the Castle precincts. But please note that at present there is normally NO PUBLIC ACCESS.

Take a detour up Little Castle Street. The Royal British Legion Building on the right was formerly Castle Street Meeting House, replaced in that function by Southernhay Congregational Church.

An old print of the Castle Chapel (by kind permission of the Librarian of the Devon and Exeter Institution).

St John the Baptist

The longest lived of the chapels in St Lawrence's parish was that dedicated to **St John the Baptist**. It stood on the south side of High Street, close to the City wall, about where Maples Furniture Shop now stands.

This chapel had its origins in a hospital or workhouse founded by the Exeter citizen William Prohume or Proden around 1170. Dedicated to St Alexius, it was situated behind St Nicholas's Priory and remained there for some fifty years. St John's hospital was founded sometime around 1230 (one source says about 1225, another 1238) and the rents, rights, fees and customs of St Alexius's were transferred to it. Bradbeer says that the hospital was built on the site of the old church of St John the Baptist, but provides no documentary corroboration. (Here's a topic for some meaty research; was there really a church there before the hospital? Rose-Troup cites an ordinance of Bishop Quivil dated Wednesday after the Feast of St Bartholomew 1287 uniting the parishes of St John and St Lawrence, but simply concludes that the hospital was counted as a parish at that time.) The hospital retained the rare privilege of burial within its precincts, "that the clergy and poor brethren might sleep their long sleep where their peaceful days had been passed".

St John's served as a priory, almshouse, school and hospital. The priory was the last in Exeter to succumb to the Dissolution, not surrendering until 1540. The buildings then reverted to secular use. In 1629, the chancel of the old hospital church was turned into a chapel for the recently established grammar school; the nave was divided horizontally, the upper half being used for instruction, while the lower half was subsequently let off as a wool hall. The early pages of Bradbeer contain several other fascinating details of the establishment's history. Jenkins describes the chapel as "small and neat, with an arched roof and gothic windows". There was a gallery at the west end accommodating the school's boarders, with a private passage to the Master's house and school. The chapel was sold in 1878 to enable a new General Post Office to be built on the site.

St John's Hospital and Chapel.

St Bartholomew

Across the road from St John's chapel, possibly within the East Gate, there once stood a chapel dedicated to **St Bartholomew**. Palerna's grant mentions it. It appears to have been annexed to St John's, perhaps in 1243. It has been suggested that there was a building between the chapel and the gate itself, but recent archaeological evidence indicates that the chapel was actually in the gate. The fact that on 26 September 1459 the inner part of the gate collapsed taking with it the chapel would seem to add weight to this view. Some rebuilding must have taken place, as there is a record of a new altar hanging being purchased in 1537. There seems to be no record of St Bartholomew's final demise; perhaps it was a victim of the Dissolution, when various religious establishments in addition to monasteries were abolished, or of the Reformation a few years later.

St Sidwell

Now let us leave the confines of the old City Walls and continue up the north side of Sidwell Street, to the church dedicated to this local Saint, Latin name Sativola, on the site of her martyrdom. Although outside the wall, this was one of the parish churches designated in 1222, and it is thought to pre-date the Norman Conquest. By the end of the thirteenth century, probably for reasons of economy, the parish was joined with those of St Michael Heavitree and St David. St Michael's became the mother church, curiously, because St Sidwell's was probably the older, and had its own saint, shrine and well. The present church is claimed as the sixth on the site, the earliest dating from the sixth century. The building Jenkins describes replaced its predecessor in 1437. It had a nave, chancel, two aisles and galleries and a tower. The church served as a prison after the civil war. A new marble altar piece was added in 1801, and the two galleries were rebuilt in semi-circular form in 1804. Jenkins mentions a "gothic screen lately new painted and gilt". In spite of these improvements, the church was almost wholly rebuilt in 1812 (retaining some of its old pillars and the tower) and it reopened on 26 September 1813. Internally, there were still the nave, chancel, north and south aisles and galleries all round. The tower was provided with a spire with a frame of deal, boarded and covered with sheet copper from one of Nelson's men-of-war broken up at Devonport dockyard.

This spire was given a weathercock, measuring 2 feet 9 inches from beak to tail, and some 2 feet 6 inches in height. It was one of the oldest representations of a crowing cock used as a weather vane in this country, and probably anywhere. Ironically, it is the tenth-century Exeter Book that refutes any claim to its being the first; therein is a riddle to which the answer is "weathercock". Also, Winchester cathedral is known to have had one in the tenth century. St Sidwell's weathercock was made in 1484, and stood on a low spire on the north tower of the Cathedral. The spire was removed in 1752, and the cock found its way to St Sidwell's at the 1812 rebuilding. St Sidwell's spire was condemned as unsafe and demolished in 1900, and the tower returned to its earlier appearance.

I have been unable to ascertain the fate of the cock. Was it put back on the rebuilt tower to be destroyed in the blitz, or was it stored somewhere after the 1900 rebuilding? Any information would be much appreciated.

St Sidwell's was badly damaged in the blitz of 1942. Worship continued in a Nissen hut until the new church was ready. Rebuilding started in 1957, and while regret has been expressed that the damaged tower was demolished rather than repaired (war damage compensation being inadequate to meet the cost), at least some Victorian gothic woodwork from the old church was re-used – see *Sidwell Street*, No 5 in this series, pp.22-4. On p.14 of the same booklet, lively goings-on in the 1840s in connection with the introduction of what the staunchly Protestant locals regarded as Catholic practices are summarised.

While in this part of the city, have a look at Sidwell Street Methodist Church, a pioneer in the use of reinforced brick and concrete – again see *Sidwell Street*, pp.24-5.

St Sidwell's, pre-war.

St James's church. A daughter church of St Sidwell, this was also destroyed in the war.

Bedford Chapel

Come back inside the line of the old walls, along the south side of High Street, and pause at the junction with Bedford Street. About half-way along towards Southernhay West, there had been, until 1539, a Dominican Friary with a chapel. The site became a town house for the Earls of Bedford, known as Bedford House. This in turn was demolished, to the regret of those who knew the building, in 1773, and the speculative development of what became known as Bedford Circus started. This began as a crescent, comparable with those in Bath. It became a circus some years later when the other half was completed. Bedford Chapel was on the western side opposite the present post office, approximately on the site of the shop at No. 30 Bedford Street. It was erected as a proprietary chapel in 1832 when all the other churches in the city were closed due to an outbreak of cholera. Because of the cholera, Bishop Philpotts had gone to live temporarily in Torquay, and he had to obtain special permission to enter the city in order to consecrate it. Bedford Chapel apparently had no dedication, and having no parish, its registers were incorporated with those of St Stephen's. The chapel was on street level at the front, with a classical portico and Ionic columns at either side of the door, but the back entrance gave on to the 'parish' rooms and schoolrooms, the chapel appearing to be upstairs. Because it stood on the west side of the Circus, its entrance, complete with very small font was at the east end, the altar at the west (!). Galleries ran round three sides of the building. Cresswell suggests that "the original designer was not sure whether he was building a church or a theatre, or having been asked to design both at the same time, got his plans mixed". The only merit she sees in the building is that "it preserves a certain sacredness to a locality where for many centuries the Dominican Convent of Black Friars never omitted the sounds of prayer and praise through all the hours of day and night".

The first incumbent of Bedford Chapel was the Revd William Scoresby. Whether the unusual alignment bugged him or not is pure conjecture, but we do know that he was an active scientist who worked out a way of correcting discrepancies that the recently-introduced iron hulls of ships were causing to their compasses. For further details of Mr Scoresby's remarkable career, see the *Dictionary of National Biography*, vol 17.

An indication of the life-style of another of Bedford Chapel's ministers, the Revd W Jackson, can be gleaned from *Pennsylvania*, No. 4 in this series, p.34. There is reproduced a poster for an auction of the contents of his residence No. 2, Pennsylvania. Many of the articles had come from the Palace of Fontainebleau, and there was much fine wine. One wonders if the apparent affluence of Mr Jackson was typical of the incumbents of Bedford Chapel. Bedford Circus was certainly a very fashionable area. It used to be known as the "Bonnet Shop", with so many ladies to be seen displaying their new hats.

Bedford Circus and its chapel were badly damaged by Hitler's bombs in May 1942 and although Hoskins claims that they "could have been rescued and rebuilt had the good will been present" the remains were eventually cleared in October 1946. The Bishop granted the congregation permission to use St Stephen's church, where a stop on the organ became a memorial to the last priest-in-charge of the Bedford Chapel, the Revd H C Brenton. The congregation became established there, and continued the Evangelical ministry formerly exercised in Bedford Chapel.

Bedford Chapel.

St Stephen

Pass down High Street and under **St Stephen's Bow**, having inspected the church itself. Can you believe the story that some 1,500 Parliamentary soldiers sent out of London by General Monk when he was trying to restore the monarchy were lodged in St Stephen's in the 1660s?

St Catherine

Continue along Catherine Street to the remains of **St Catherine's Chapel**. This formerly served St Catherine's Almshouses, founded by John Stevens, a canon of the Cathedral, some time around 1456. The chapel reverted to secular use in the seventeenth-century; in 1841 for example it was a carpenter's workshop. In 1894 Lady Hotham provided the funds to restore the buildings, and the property was transferred to the Church Army. From 1897 it was used as a men's hostel. St Catherine's became another victim of the blitz, a partial victim, but too far damaged to be restored. It was left unrepaired as a war memorial.

St Martin

A little further along, **St Martin's**, with its curiously asymmetrical interior and tower which was formerly outside its parish, in Dean and Chapter territory, must be visited. St Martin's medieval parish boundaries were particularly bizarre. Basically, the parish comprised properties on the south side of High Street, but towards its western end, the boundary crossed the road to include two properties on the north side as well.

St Petrock

The nearby **St Petrock's** (access from High Street) also presents many points of interest. Originally running conventionally east-west, as it expanded southwards (the only direction possible) at various times to accommodate ever-increasing congregations, it eventually became wider than it was long, so the decision was taken to re-orientate the internal arrangements on a south-north alignment. In 1994, the southern portion was converted into a drop-in centre for the homeless. This just left the original northernmost part of the building still serving as a church on its original east-west alignment. Thus our post-card view of the interior is one that is unlikely to be seen again.

St Petrock's has what is believed to be the lightest peal of six bells in the country. Brice tells us that at 8,12 and 4 o'clock St Petrock's chimes played "Sternhold's queer old tune", described in the poem itself as "snip-snap Musick", of the fourth psalm.

The interior of St Petrock's church before its recent conversion to a drop-in centre.

Now let's go back into the Cathedral Close. Our tour is not quite finished, for we are still but a stone's throw away from four other chapels mentioned in one or other of our two thirteenth-century documents referred to at the beginning.

St Peter Minor

St Peter Minor was an ancient chapel standing behind a house in High Street opposite the Guildhall, which locates it somewhere in the north-west edge of the Cathedral Close. It was used early in the thirteenth century by a guild known as the City of Exeter and Kalendar Brethren, and was still a religious establishment in 1281. The site was vacant by 1285, and by about 1308 the residence of one J Perer stood there.

Ss Simon and Jude

A chapel dedicated to **Saints Simon and Jude** is mentioned in Bishop Marshal's ordinance, and Rose-Troup provides documentary evidence that it was still there in 1265. It seems to have been located between St Peter Minor and St Petrock.

St Edward the King

Palerna's grant mentions a chapel dedicated to **St Edward the King** identified by Rose-Troup as King Edward the Martyr, c.962-978 or 979. This probably stood near the north-west corner of the Cathedral, to become what later accounts describe simply as the Charnel Chapel. It seems to have been a Chantry Chapel for Bishop Stapledon in the fourteenth century and was altered or even rebuilt for that purpose in the late 1320s. John Leland in Exeter in or about 1538 mentions the Charnel Chapel, but it had disappeared not many years later.

St Michael

Bishop Marshal's ordinance lists a chapel dedicated to **St Michael**. When the residence for the first Dean was built in or soon after 1225, the chapel stood beside it. Some time later, when the Deanery was enlarged, the chapel was included within the walls and became an oratory for the Dean's own use.

And here we conclude our tour of the old city and its churches. We may recall that in the suburbs, St Michael's Heavitree was certainly there in 1153 and that there were in its parish chapels dedicated to Saints Clarus, Anne, Mary, Loye (ie Eligius), James, as well as others mentioned below, and the undedicated chapel at Livery Dole (see Orme, *The medieval chapels…*). We should mention St Michael's former daughter churches which are also of ancient lineage, the twelfth-century St Leonard's and the originally Celtic St David's, both now in their fourth manifestations. Mention of St David's reminds us that there was until the seventeenth century the remnant, at least, of a chapel dedicated to St Clement somewhere in the area now occupied by the railway station. It was still there in 1537 but apparently in ruins by 1571. St Thomas's, once occupying a position at the west end of the Exe bridge, mirroring that of St Edmund's on the city side, was founded in the thirteenth century. And of post-medieval churches, St James's was destroyed in the war and the new St James's built some distance away, (see *Pennsylvania*, No 4 in this series, p. 43). The nineteenth-century church of St Matthew, now in a parish united with that of St Sidwell, is still in use, and further away, St Marks in Pinhoe Road, built in 1935, now houses the bells (recast in 1950) that were once in St George's and St John's.

St David's, St Leonard's and Heavitree each have a booklet in this series devoted to their area. These include basic details about the places of worship, but it is hoped to provide fuller information in a later volume.

Bibliography

The following publications have been drawn on frequently and most are often referred to in the text:-

BRADBEER, Doris *Joyful schooldays*. Exeter: Sydney Lee, 1973

BRICE, Andrew *The Mobiad: or, battle of the voice. An heroic-comic poem… being a description of an Exeter election…* . London: T Davies, 1770
[But note that the election concerned took place in 1738. The poem contains many notes added by Brice, so the work as a whole gives glimpses of the city in both years].

CHERRY, Bridget and PEVSNER, Nikolaus *The buildings of England: Devon. Harmondsworth*. Penguin, 2nd ed 1989.

*CRESSWELL, Beatrix *Exeter churches*. Exeter: James G Commin, 1908

Exeter Cathedral: a celebration . Exeter: Dean and Chapter of Exeter, 1991

FREEMAN, E A *Historic towns: Exeter*. London: Longman, Green and Co., 1887

HELE'S SCHOOL HISTORICAL SOCIETY *Exeter then and now*. Exeter: A Wheaton and Company, [1945?]

HOSKINS, W G *Two thousand years in Exeter*. Exeter: James Townsend and Sons Limited, 2nd impression 1963

JENKINS, Alexander *The history and description of the city of Exeter*. Exeter: P Hedgeland, 1806

LITTLE, Bryan *Portrait of Exeter*. London: Robert Hale, 1983

MacCAFFERY, Wallace T *Exeter, 1540-1640: the growth of an English county town*. Cambridge, Mass.: Harvard University Press, 1958

MELLER, Hugh *Exeter architecture*. Chichester: Phillimore, 1989

NORTHY, T J *Illustrated popular history of Exeter*. Exeter: J G Commin, 1886

ORME, Nicholas i. The medieval chapels of Heavitree. *Devon Archaeological Society Proceedings*, 49, 1991, pp.121-9
ii. The Kalendar Brethren of the city of Exeter. *Reports and Transactions of the Devon Association for the Advancement of Science*, 109, 1977, pp.153-69
iii. *Exeter Cathedral as it was*. Exeter: Devon Books, 1986.

PEVSNER, Nikolaus *The buildings of England: South Devon*. Harmondsworth: Penguin, 1952

*ROSE-TROUP, Frances *Lost chapels of Exeter*. Exeter: History of Exeter Research Group, 1923

SHARP, Thomas *Exeter phoenix*. London: Architectural Press, 1946

THOMAS, Peter and WARREN, Jacqueline. *Aspects of Exeter*. Plymouth: Baron Jay, 1980

* The work of Beatrix Cresswell and Frances Rose-Troup contributes so much to our story that a little biographical information about them follows.

Beatrix Feodore Clara Augusta Grace Cresswell, 1862-1940, inherited her love of historical subjects and aptitude for Latin and Greek from her father Richard Cresswell, a graduate of St John's College, Oxford, a well-known coach and some time curate-in-charge at Salcombe Regis. She had an interest in heraldry from an early age, and designed coats of arms for all her dolls. Miss Cresswell lived in Exeter for many years. She published numerous books and articles on Devon and Exeter subjects, and also a play set in old Exeter, *White rose and golden broom*. It is said that she visited every church in Devon twice in the course of her researches. She was a member of the Council of the Devonshire Association. Miss Cresswell died on 16 February 1940, and was buried in the Higher Cemetery after a memorial service at the cathedral.

Frances Batchelder Rose-Troup (née James), 1859-1942, was born in Philadelphia and brought up in Cambridge, Massachussetts. She settled with her mother in Rockbeare around 1887, and in January 1889 married John Rose Troup (apparently without the hyphen). He had recently returned from Central Africa where he had been a member of H M Stanley's expedition for the relief of Emir Pasha. From about 1925, now a widow, she devoted herself to historical research, particularly on Exeter and Ottery St Mary, and became a Fellow of the Royal Historical Society. She was also a member of the Devonshire Association, and at her death, only three members had a longer span of membership. She had joined the Council of the Association in 1888, and retained her seat for the next 54 years. She died on 28 November 1942.

It is intriguing to speculate whether these two ladies, whose interests overlapped to a considerable extent and who were both Council members of the Association, ever worked together, or whether they were of the "formidable" type, and deadly rivals? Perhaps someone knows the answer to this and will inform us, but in the meantime, some lines from the obituary of Frances Rose-Troup in the *Transactions of the Devonshire Association* (no less!), 74, 1942, pp.39-40 may provide a clue: "Her researches and publications did not always meet with the full approval of other workers in the same field, but… they often suggest lines which others may follow with advantage".

Acknowledgements

My especial thanks are due to Hazel Harvey for setting up this project, and for many stories, illustrations and snippets of information; to her husband David for his many suggestions on facts and presentation; to Richard Parker for providing the map at the beginning, and to both him and Robert Sweetland for sharing their expertise with me; to Professor Nicholas Orme, whose researches have unravelled several knotty problems and provided much interesting reading; to the Curator of the Royal Albert Memorial Museum for supplying the illustration on page 9 ; to Devon County Council Libraries (Westcountry Studies Library) for supplying the illustration on page 15 ; to the Editor of the *Western Morning News* for allowing the use of the illustration on page 20 ; to the Librarian of the Devon and Exeter Institution for lending and allowing the use of the illustration on page 48, and for supplying copies of the drawings made by W G Croump 1933 - 1940 of 'Mural monuments and other items of historical and general interest to be seen in the streets of Exeter', on pages 13, 18, 25, 26, 31, 35, 37, 40 and 46 ; to Monica Hoare, whose grandfather's firm, Worth and Co., published the postcards used on pages 30 and 41; to John Fowles for permission to quote from *The French lieutenant's woman*; to the always helpful members of staff in the Westcountry Studies Library, the Devon and Exeter Institution Library and the Cathedral Library, and to Robin and Pamela Wootton for their friendship and encouragement.

Exeter Civic Society
Registered Charity No. 286932
Enquiries: 53 Thornton Hill, Exeter EX4 4NR

Notes

Notes